SHOW and TELL

Lew Maurer

Stella Maris

For Alix

Lew was VERY shy.

At school, when the teacher called on him, he got nervous. Sometimes, his face got red and it was hard to talk.

"So," the teacher continued, "one day soon, Lew will bring something from home for show and tell."

To stand in front of the class made him nervous.

He wanted to do something different than the other kids.

And then he had an idea!

The next day, Lew walked to school with a large shopping bag.

All his friends wanted to see what was in the bag, but he didn't let anyone look inside.

His teacher was surprised when he came into the classroom with his big bag.

With a big smile,

Lew reached inside the bag...

...and lifted a SNAKE over his head, so all the kids could see.

Lew was very proud of his big pet snake.

It was a friendly snake that he liked to play with.

He was so excited to show it to his class that he wasn't nervous or embarrassed.

He knew they would be surprised to see such a beautiful animal. Maybe they would like to touch it and feel its smooth scales.

He was sure they would be excited to see the snake's shiny black eyes and forked tongue that went in and out.

"Aaaaaaaaaa," screamed the little red-haired girl in front of him! She jumped up and ran out of the classroom.

All the other kids and even the teacher ran out too!

Poor Lew! Standing alone with his snake, he was sad that everyone was scared.

Then, the principal called his mother. "Mrs. Maurer," Lew could hear him say, "this is not funny. I am sending him home and he cannot come back today. Please do not let him bring his snake to school again!"

Pacific Gopher Snake

The gopher snake is non-venomous and one of the largest snakes in North America. They are found all over the United States. They eat small mammals like rats and mice but also birds, lizards, and frogs. In the wild, they will pretend to be a rattlesnake sometimes, to keep other animals and people away. Hawks, coyotes, and foxes will eat them.

Like all snakes, they are cold-blooded, which means they depend on the weather to keep their body temperature just right. They can die if they become too cold or too hot. When it's cold, they like to lay in the sunshine, and when it becomes too hot, they move into the shade or a cool place.

Gopher snakes can be nice pets because they are very clean and do not bite. It is interesting to gently hold them and feel their cool, smooth, and beautiful brown and yellow scales. They need special attention, however, so they are not popular like dogs and cats. They prefer live animals for food and need cool, clean water every day.

Show and Tell is a true story. When Lew was ten years old, he had a collection of snakes that he kept in special terrariums in his backyard. He caught his snakes in the mountains when he went there to fish for trout. When he was thirteen, he took them all back to the mountains and let them go free. His big gopher snake was his favorite.

When the principal called Lew's mother, she laughed because he only had the snake in his school for one day, and she and Lew's dad had to live with his collection of six snakes all the time!

Captain Lew
BOOK SERIES

The Bogeyman has stolen his tricycle and now Lew must be brave to get it back. But the mean Bogeyman lives in a dark basement apartment on the corner...

Lew Maurer, the son of a taxi driver, could only dream he would fall in love with boats and the sea. Years later, Captain Lew would travel thousands of miles to some of the most remote and beautiful places on our planet.

But he never forgot his childhood, and as an author, he shares his adventures of growing up in Los Angeles with the same excitement as his years at sea.

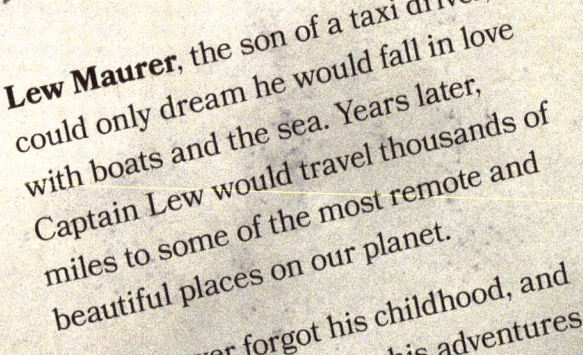

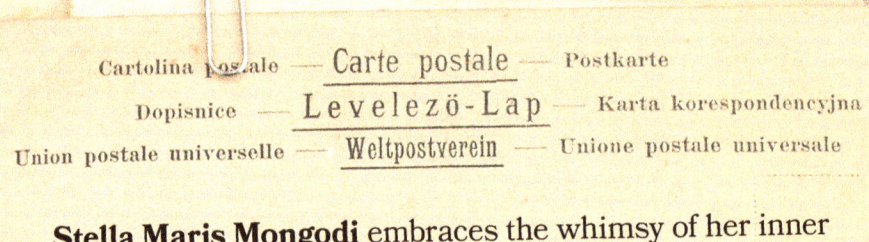

Stella Maris Mongodi embraces the whimsy of her inner child. She skates through life with zest, sewing vibrant skirts of every hue imaginable, chatting with the Death Star via her Darth Vader walkie-talkie, and forming bonds with her beloved creatures—owls, mice, and the occasional squirrel. Like Captain Lew Maurer, Stella harbors a deep-seated passion. Through her art, she voyages into fantastical realms, capturing the essence of childhood wonder with her unique flair.

Also From Captain Lew

Herman and the Princess Gull

When two unlikely characters find each other, they decide that friendship is better than instinct.

Remember that wonderful, feel-good moment when, for the first time, we see a tender, loving exchange between two animals? In *Herman and the Princess Gull*, it is especially heartwarming because the two animals would normally be life-and-death enemies.

FROM:

Compass Rose Press, USA
CompassRosePressUSA.com
Text copyright © 2024 Lew Maurer
Artwork copyright © 2024 Stella Maris Mongodi
All rights reserved

Cover and interior typesetting by Monkey C Media

No part of this publication may be reproduced, stored in a retrieval system, or transmitted in any form or by any means, electronic, mechanical, photocopying, recording, or otherwise, without written permission of the publisher, except by reviewers, who may quote brief passages in a review.

First edition
Printed in the United States of America

ISBN:
hardcover: 978-1-7335150-8-5
paperback: 978-1-7335150-9-2
ebook: 979-8-9918786-0-9

LCCN: 2024923214

www.ingramcontent.com/pod-product-compliance
Lightning Source LLC
Chambersburg PA
CBHW061123170426
43209CB00013B/1651